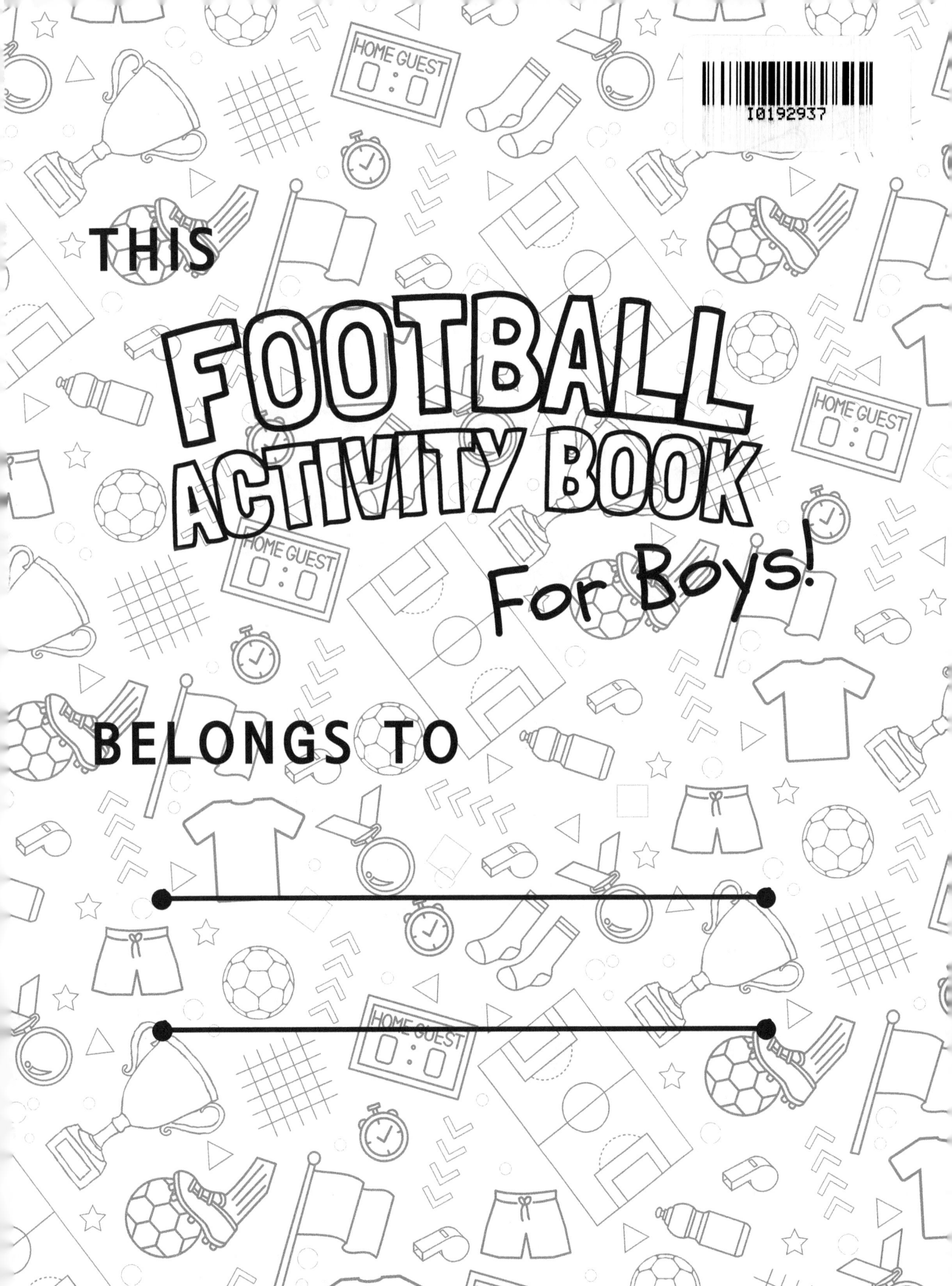

EVERYTHING STARTS WITH A DREAM

stop

Juggle

kick

FIND-A-WORD

WORD CAN BE FOUND HORIZONZAL, VERTICAL, BACKWARDS, FORWARDS AND DIAGONAL

```
U A M I D F I E L D E R O N E T O U C H
F O R M A T I O N D D T A C T I C S S D
S C I S S O R K I C K M G N H J S V E E
H S U S U B S T I T U T E T C I H O M F
V S C H A L F T I M E M I W K U P L I E
O F F S I D E C M C A M D Y H D U L F N
N T A C K L E J F N M A T C H I Z E I D
S P Q S B K T H R O W I N R T V S Y N E
F L O B S T R U C T I O N L K E A T A R
K W I I V I O S F O R W A R D I T K L J
M R G C E T S G Y N I N J U R Y T I M E
D F R Y M A R T W I N G E R B R A C E U
O O O C P A F O U L S O F C K I C K F R
V O U L S T R I K E R A I L O K K O I O
B T P E S W E K P H K L N K A R I F X P
R B V K C Y E L L O W C A R D G N F T E
B A I I O P K E R E S U L T S D G E U A
S L K C R Z I R P O S T C P L A Y E R J
K L E K E N C P D E L I V E R Y G R E A
X D H C Q Y K Q U A R T E R F I N A L R
```

LIST OF WORDS

WORD CAN BE FOUND HORIZONZAL, VERTICAL, BACKWARDS, FORWARDS AND DIAGONAL

ASSIST
ATTACKING
BICYCLE KICK
BRACE
CHIP
COMMIT
CORNER
DECOY
DEFENDER
DELIVERY
DIVE
DRIBBLE
EUROPE
FINAL
FIXTURE
FLAG
FOOTBALL
FORMATION

FORWARD
FOUL
FREE KICK
GROUP
HALF TIME
INJURY TIME
KICK
KICKOFF
KIT
MARK
MATCH
MIDFIELDER
NIL
OBSTRUCTION
OFFSIDE
ONE TOUCH
OWN GOAL
PASS
PLAYER

POST
QUARTER FINAL
RESULTS
SAVE
SCISSOR KICK
SCORE
SEMI FINAL
STRIKER
SUBSTITUTE
SWEEPER
TACKLE
TACTICS
THROW IN
TOURNAMENT
VOLLEY
WHISTLE
WINGER
YELLOW CARD

"Learn from the losses, Celebrate the Wins!"

referee

whistle

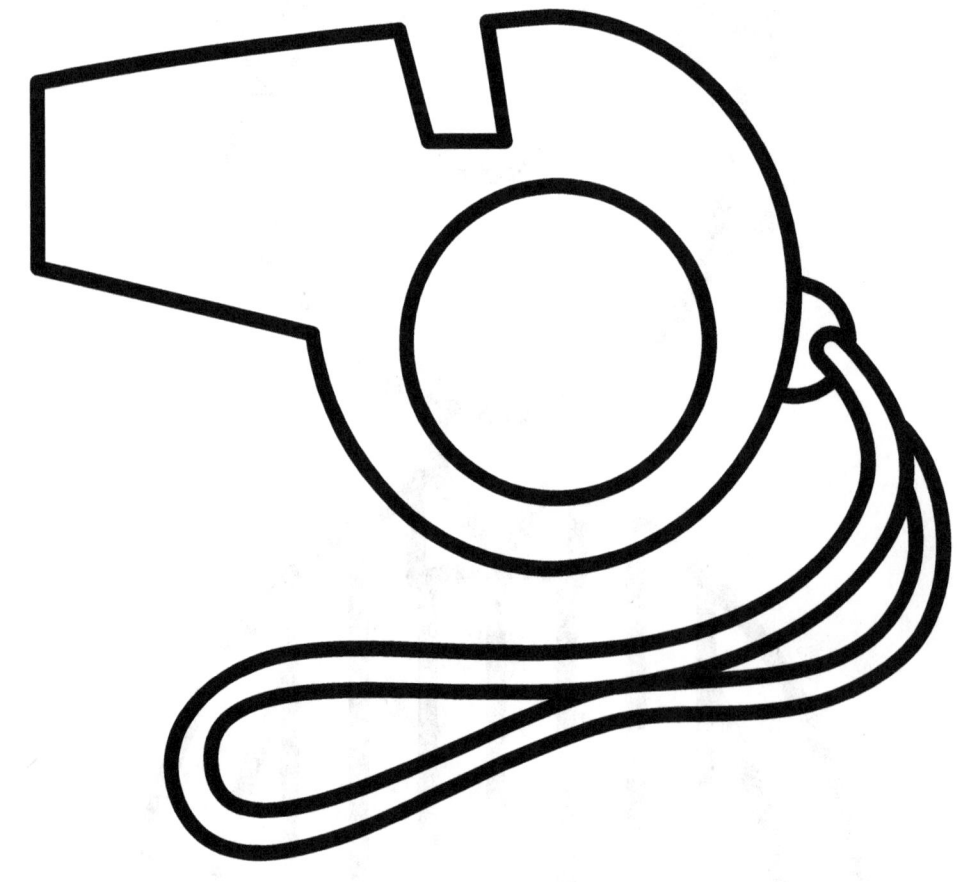

SPOT THE FOOTBALL

HOW MANY FOOTBALLS CAN YOU FIND?

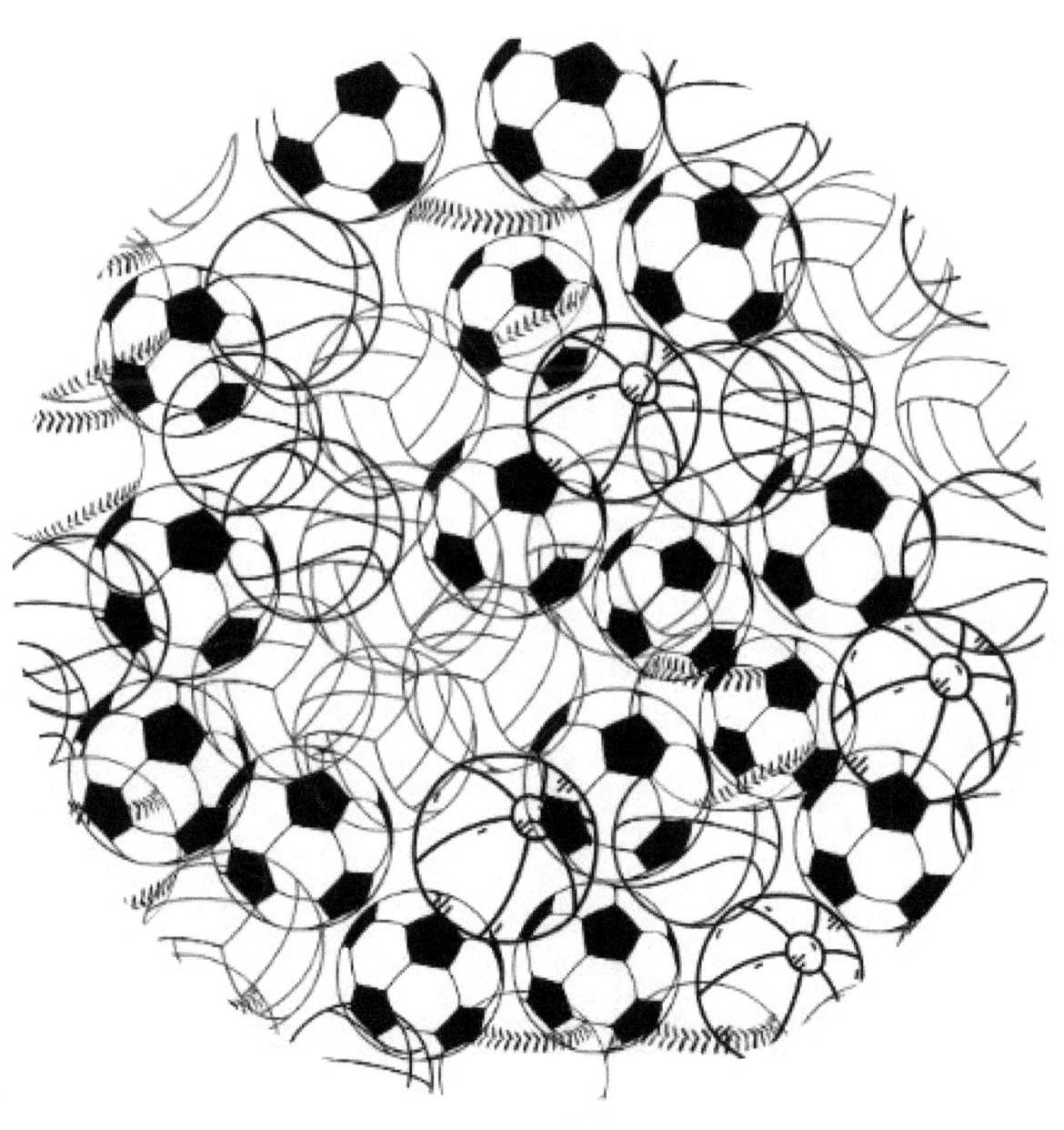

DRAW YOUR FAVOURITE PLAYER

stadium

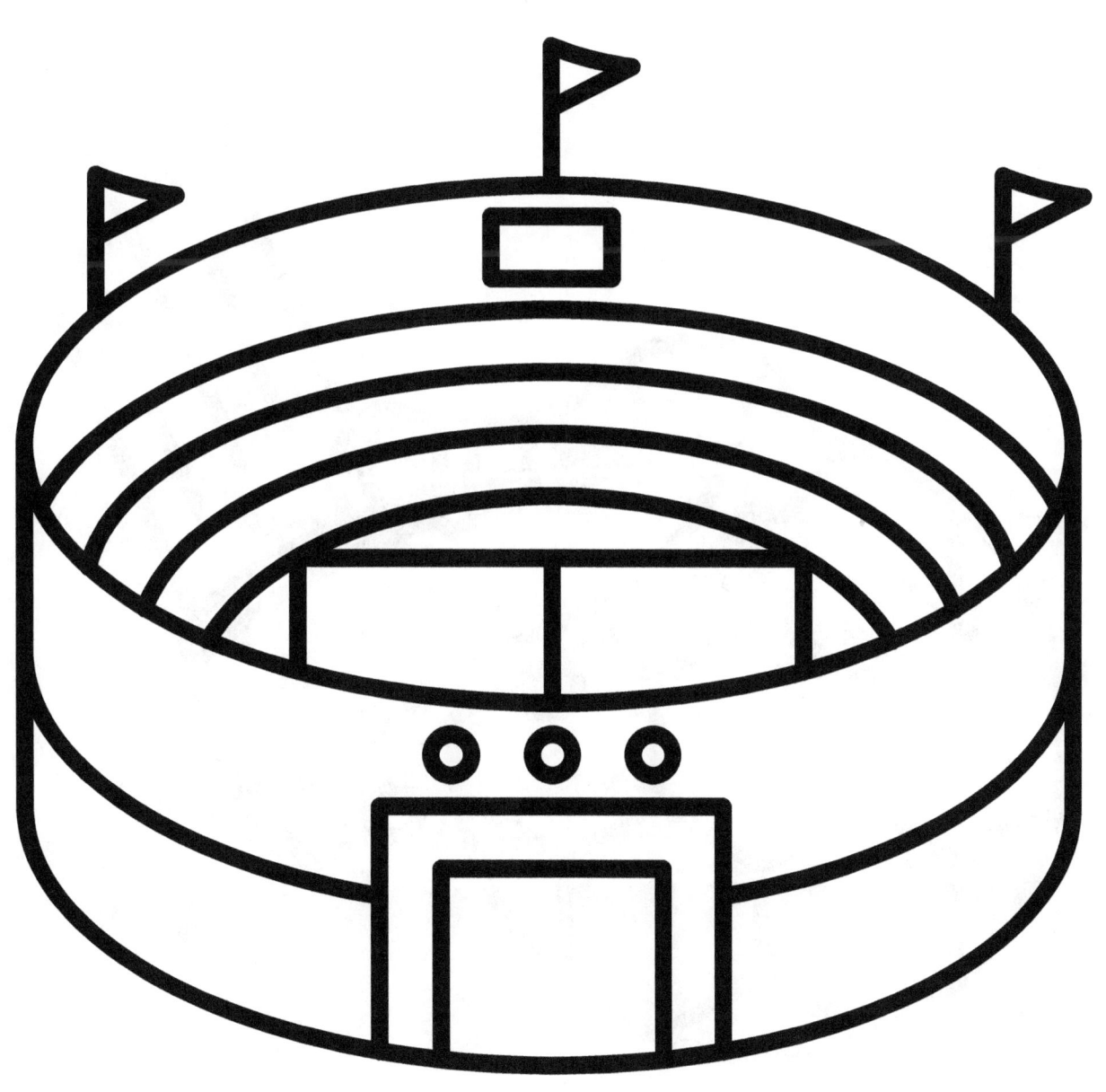

boot

gloves

goal

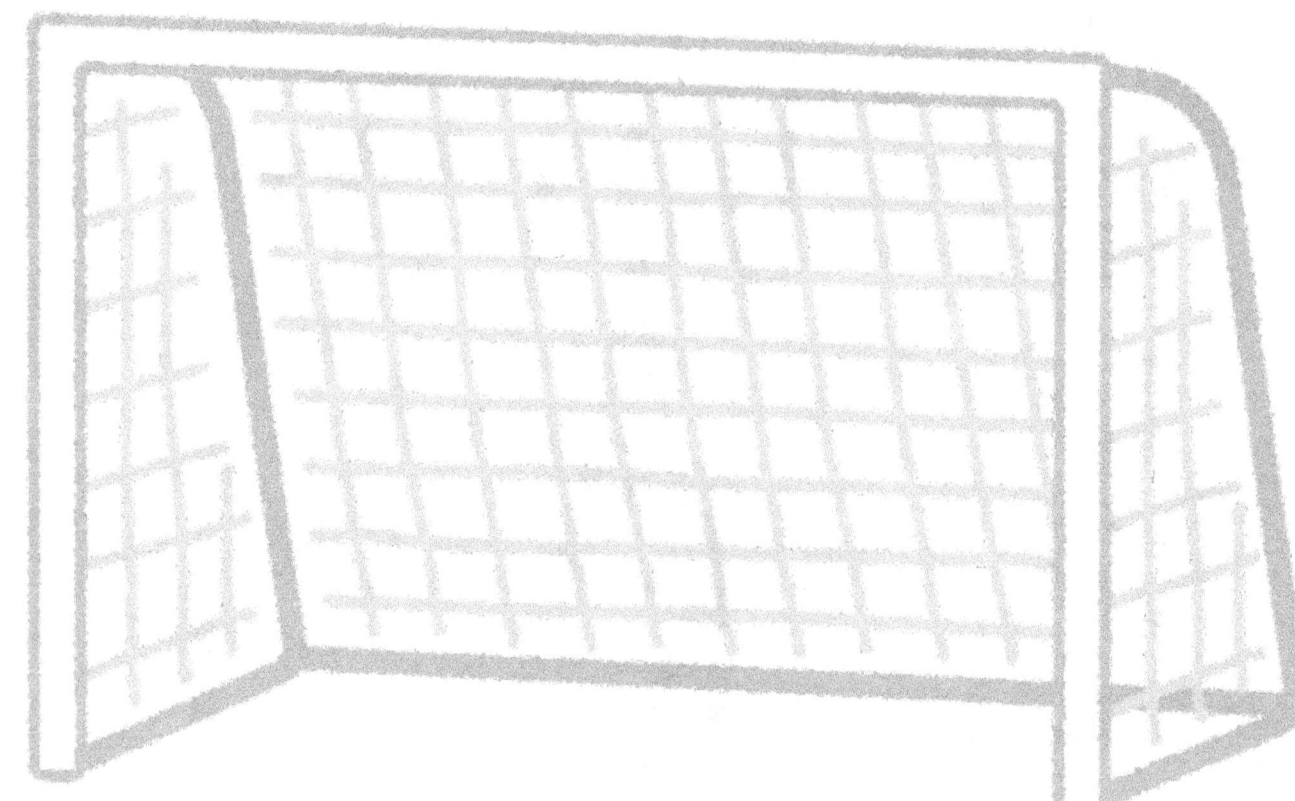

SCORE THE GOAL!

WEAVE YOUR WAY THROUGH THE MAZE TO SCORE THE GOAL

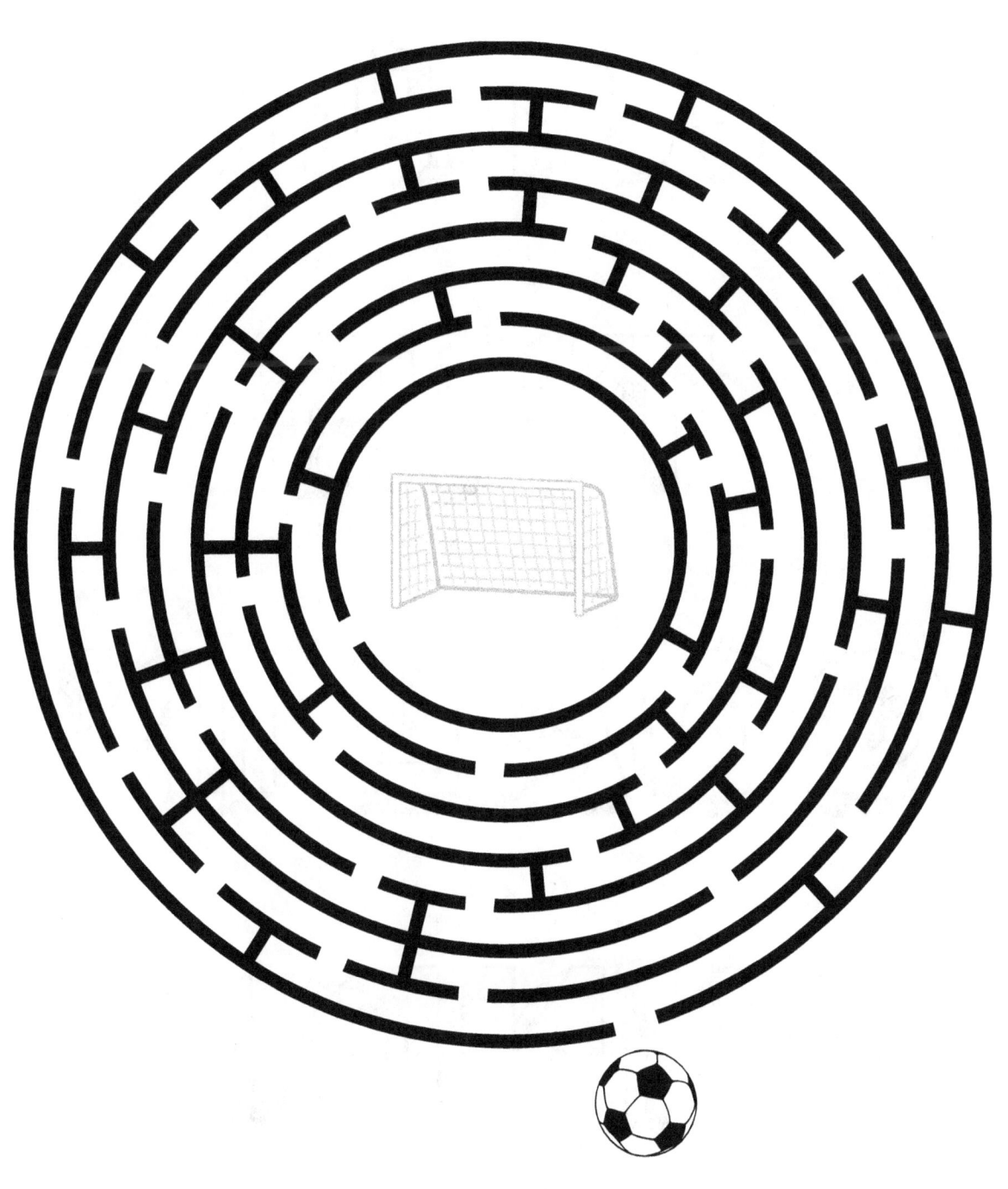

"PLAY WITH THE GOAL IN MIND!"

cards

heel

CROSSWORD

USE THE CLUES TO FILL IN THE CROSSWORD

CROSSWORD CLUES

ACROSS:

1. A PLAYER'S SHIRT
5. WHEN BOTH TEAMS SCORE THE SAME NUMBER OF GOALS AT THE END OF THE GAME
6. THE PLAYERS KICK THIS
7. THE RESULT GIVEN TO THE TEAM WHEN THEY SCORE THE MOST GOALS
10. THE PERSON WHO BLOWS THE WHISTLE
11. WHEN A PLAYER HITS THE BALL WITH THEIR HEAD
13. SOMETIMES THE BALL HITS THIS INSTEAD OF GOING INTO THE NET
15. WHEN A PLAYER SCORES 3 GOALS IN ONE GAME
17. A GROUP OF PLAYERS BELONGING TO THE SAME COUNTRY
18. THE TEAM RUN ON HERE

DOWN:

2. PLAYERS THROW THE BALL IN FROM HERE
3. THE END OF THE MATCH
4. THE PLAYER THAT CAN USE THEIR HANDS TO STOP THE OTHER TEAM FROM SCORING
8. A PLAYER GETS SENT OFF WHEN THEY RECEIVE ONE OF THESE
9. WHEN A PLAYER GETS FOULED INSIDE THE BOX
12. A PLAYER'S FOOTWEAR
14. WHEN A TEAM WINS THIS MATCH THEY QUALIFY FOR THE FINAL
16. WHAT ONE TEAM DOES TO BEGIN THE GAME
19. WHEN THE BALL GOES INTO THE NET
20. THE PLAYERS SING A NATIONS SONG BEFORE EACH GAME

ball

TRACE THE WORD AND MATCH THE PICTURE

jersey

boot

socks

shorts

SCORE THE GOAL!

WEAVE YOUR WAY THROUGH THE MAZE TO SCORE THE GOAL

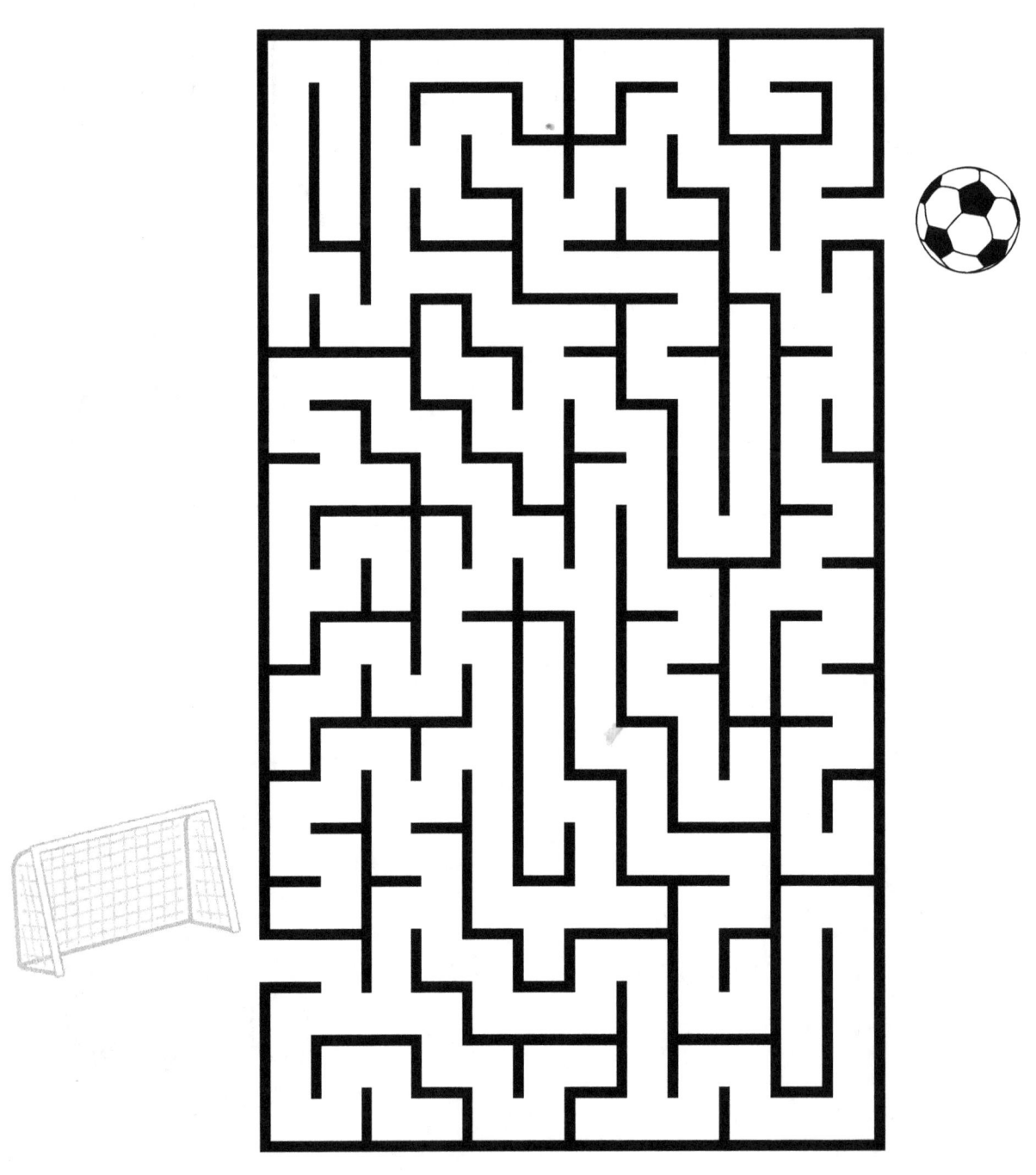

tricks

control

header

"SOMETIMES YOU HAVE TO PLAY BACKWARDS TO MOVE FORWARDS!"

Jersey

shorts

Socks

Score

crowd

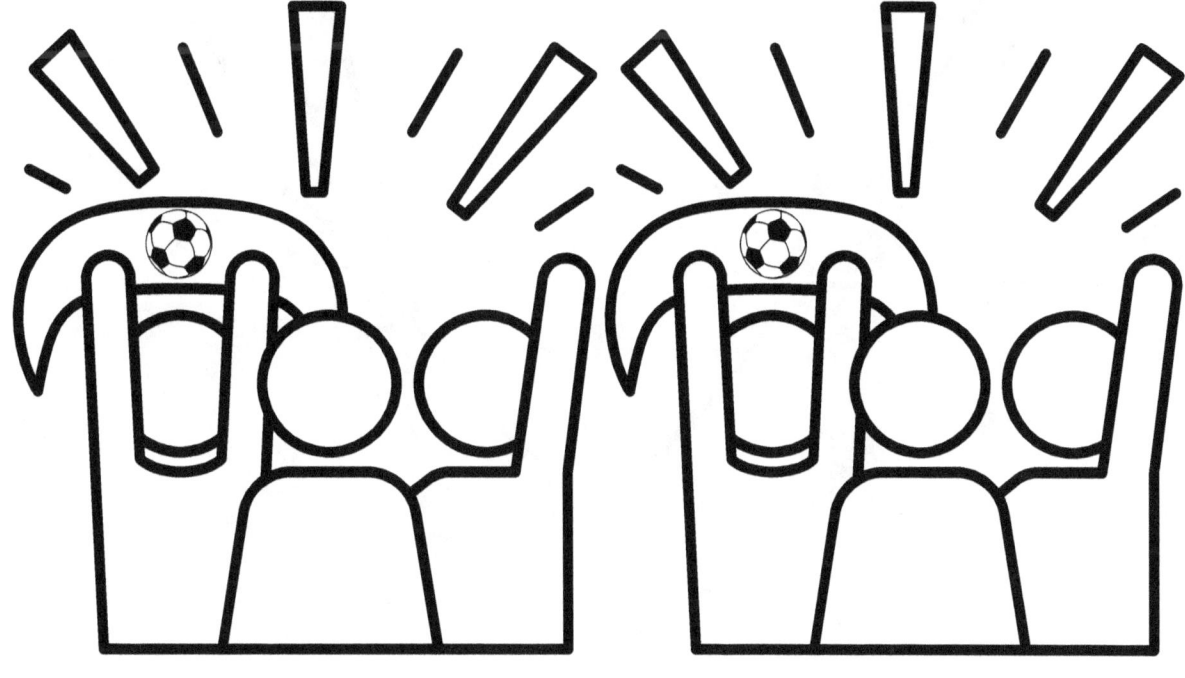

Winners

"Teamwork makes the dream work!"

TRACE THE WORD AND MATCH THE PICTURE

referee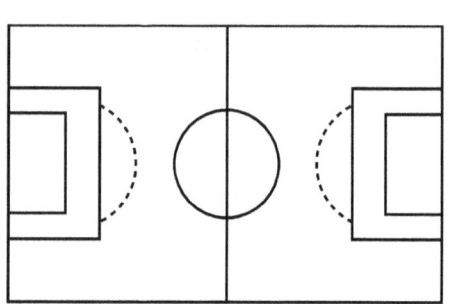

whistle

pitch

medal

medal

BUILD-A-JERSEY

(FRONT)

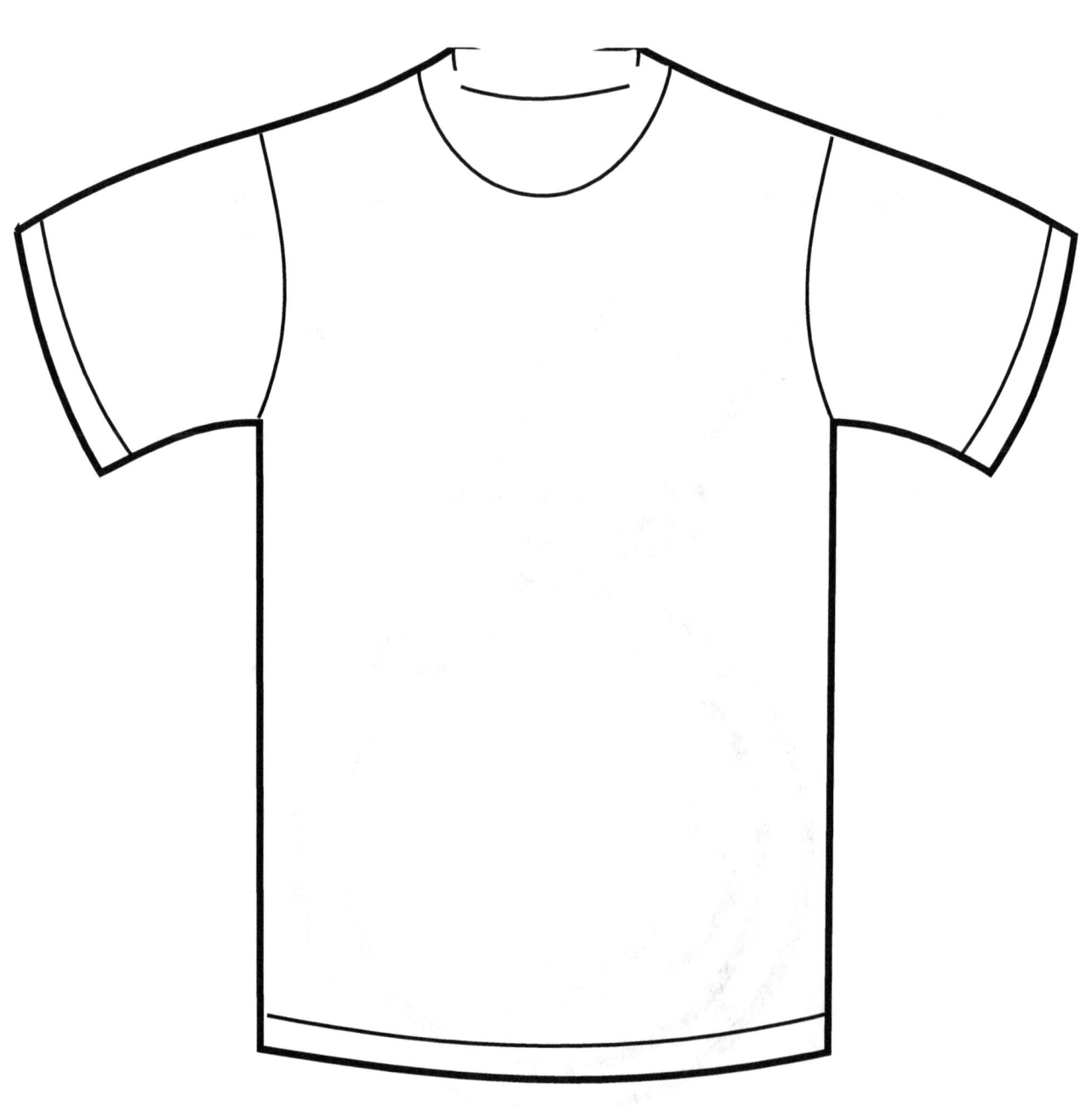

BUILD-A-JERSEY

(BACK)

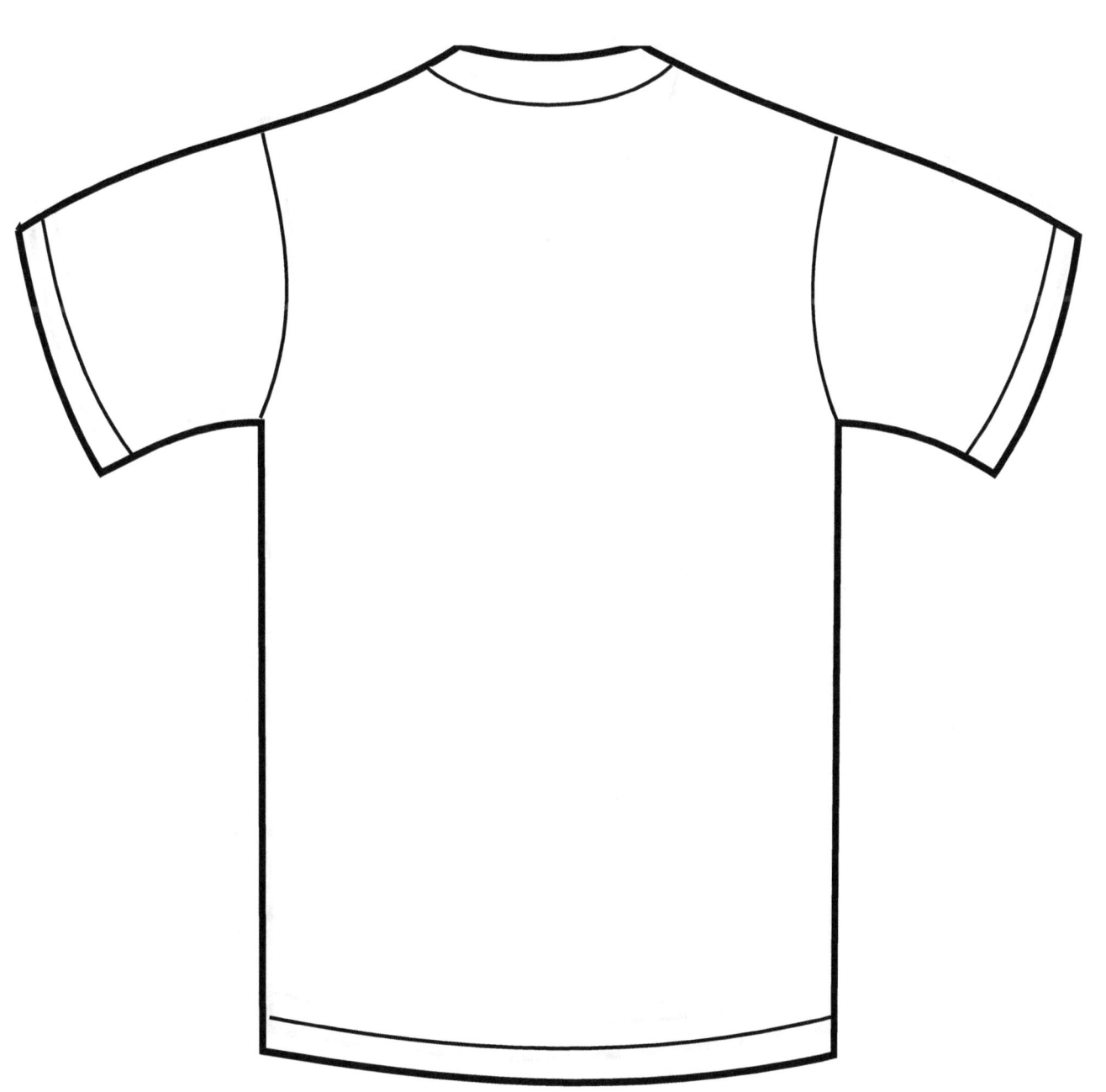

BUILD-A-JERSEY

(FRONT)

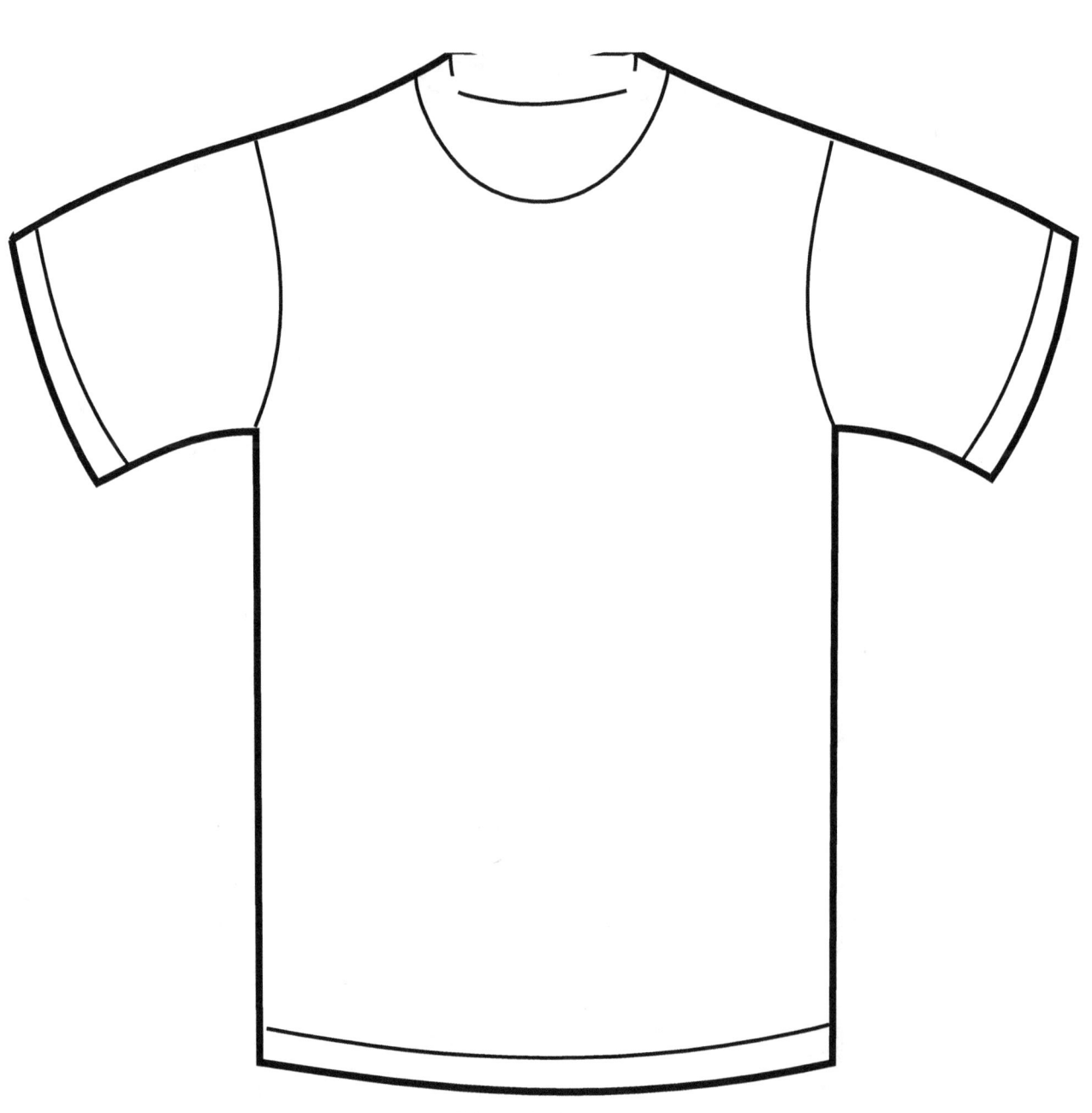

BUILD-A-JERSEY

(BACK)

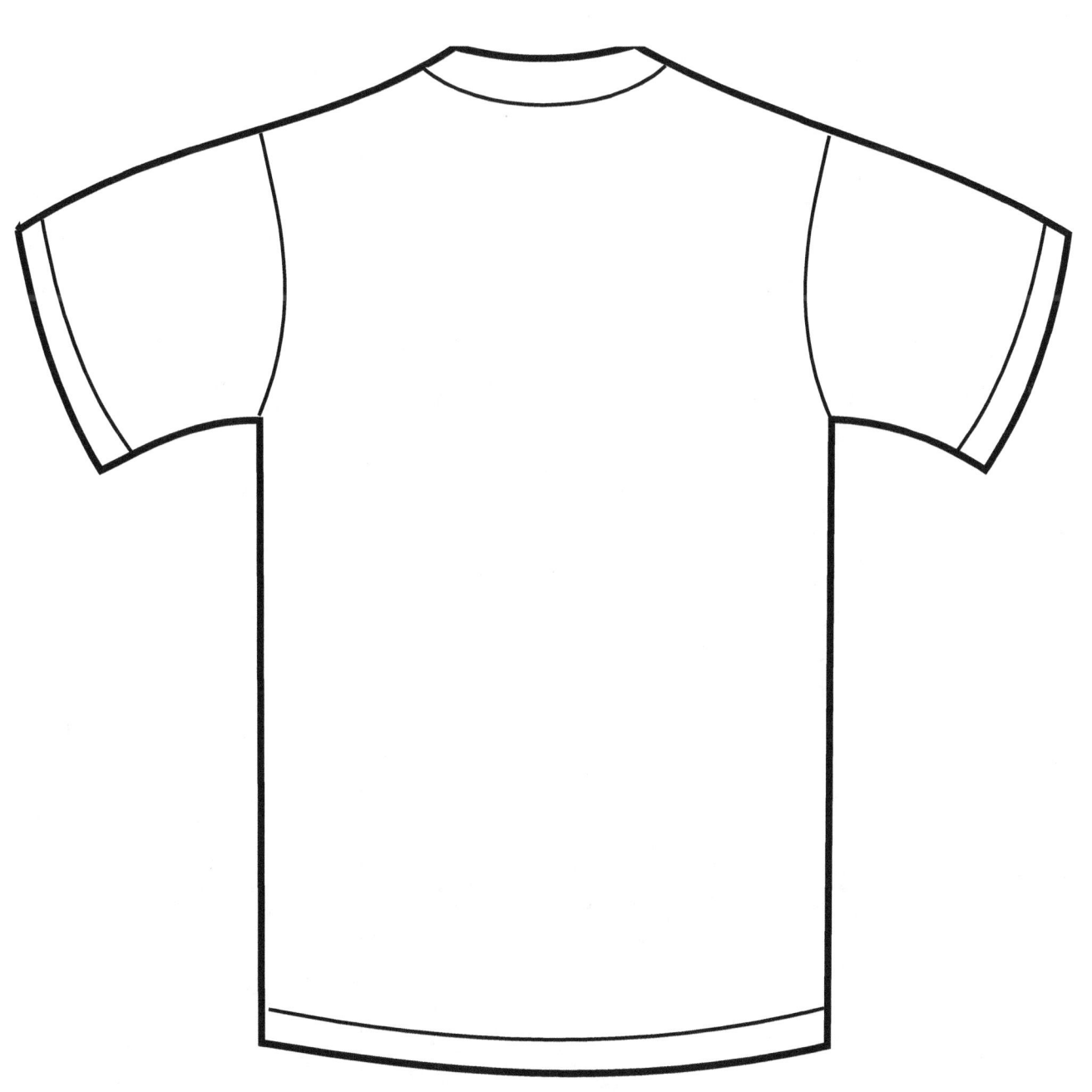

THIS PAGE INTENTIONALLY LEFT BLANK
FOR BUILD-A-JERSEY ACTIVITY

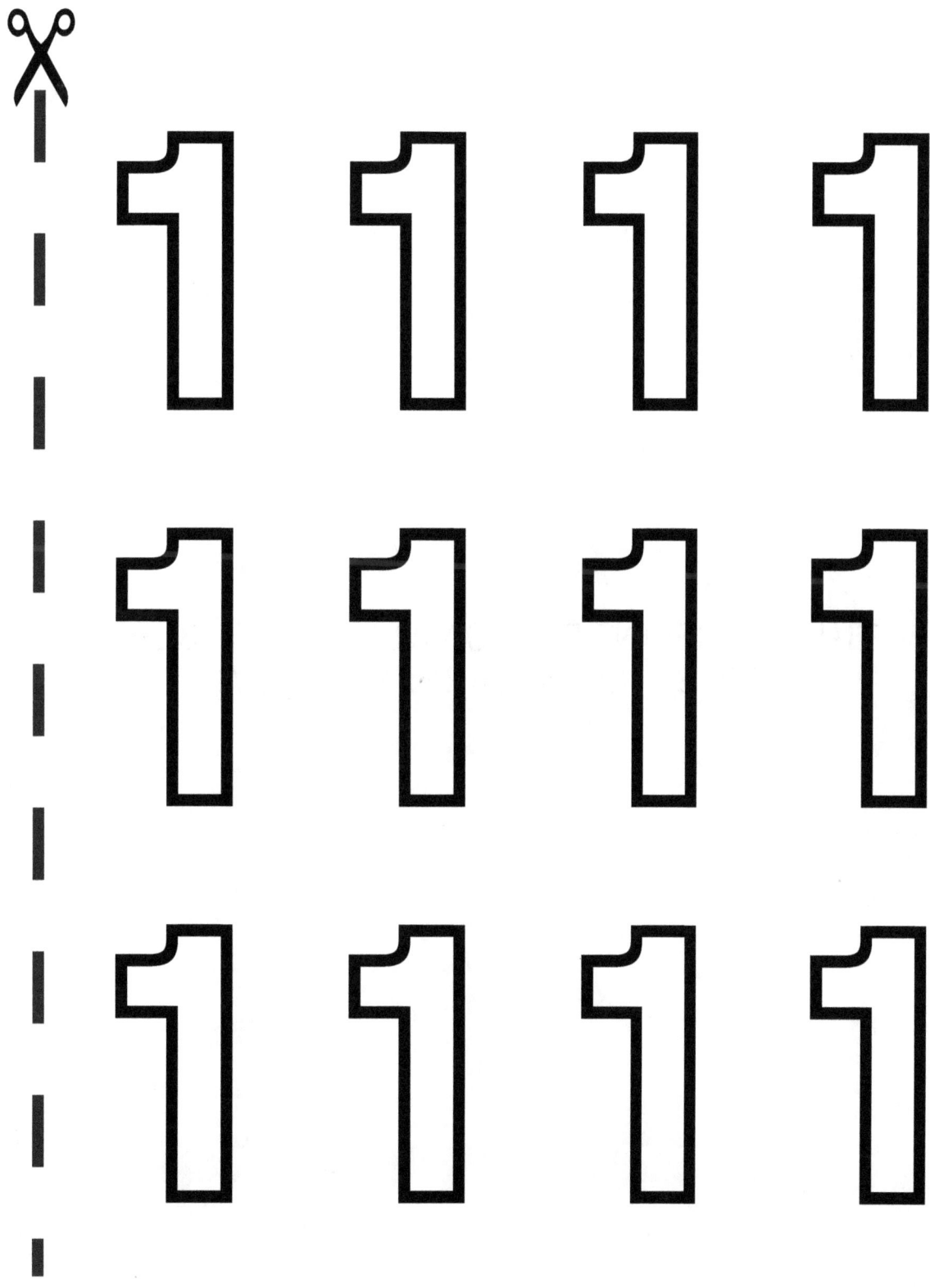

THIS PAGE INTENTIONALLY LEFT BLANK
FOR BUILD-A-JERSEY ACTIVITY

2	2	2
2	2	2
2	2	2

THIS PAGE INTENTIONALLY LEFT BLANK
FOR BUILD-A-JERSEY ACTIVITY

3	3	3
3	3	3
3	3	3

THIS PAGE INTENTIONALLY LEFT BLANK
FOR BUILD-A-JERSEY ACTIVITY

4 4 4

4 4 4

4 4 4

THIS PAGE INTENTIONALLY LEFT BLANK
FOR BUILD-A-JERSEY ACTIVITY

5 5 5

5 5 5

5 5 5

THIS PAGE INTENTIONALLY LEFT BLANK
FOR BUILD-A-JERSEY ACTIVITY

6 6 6
6 6 6
6 6 6

THIS PAGE INTENTIONALLY LEFT BLANK
FOR BUILD-A-JERSEY ACTIVITY

7 7 7

7 7 7

7 7 7

THIS PAGE INTENTIONALLY LEFT BLANK
FOR BUILD-A-JERSEY ACTIVITY

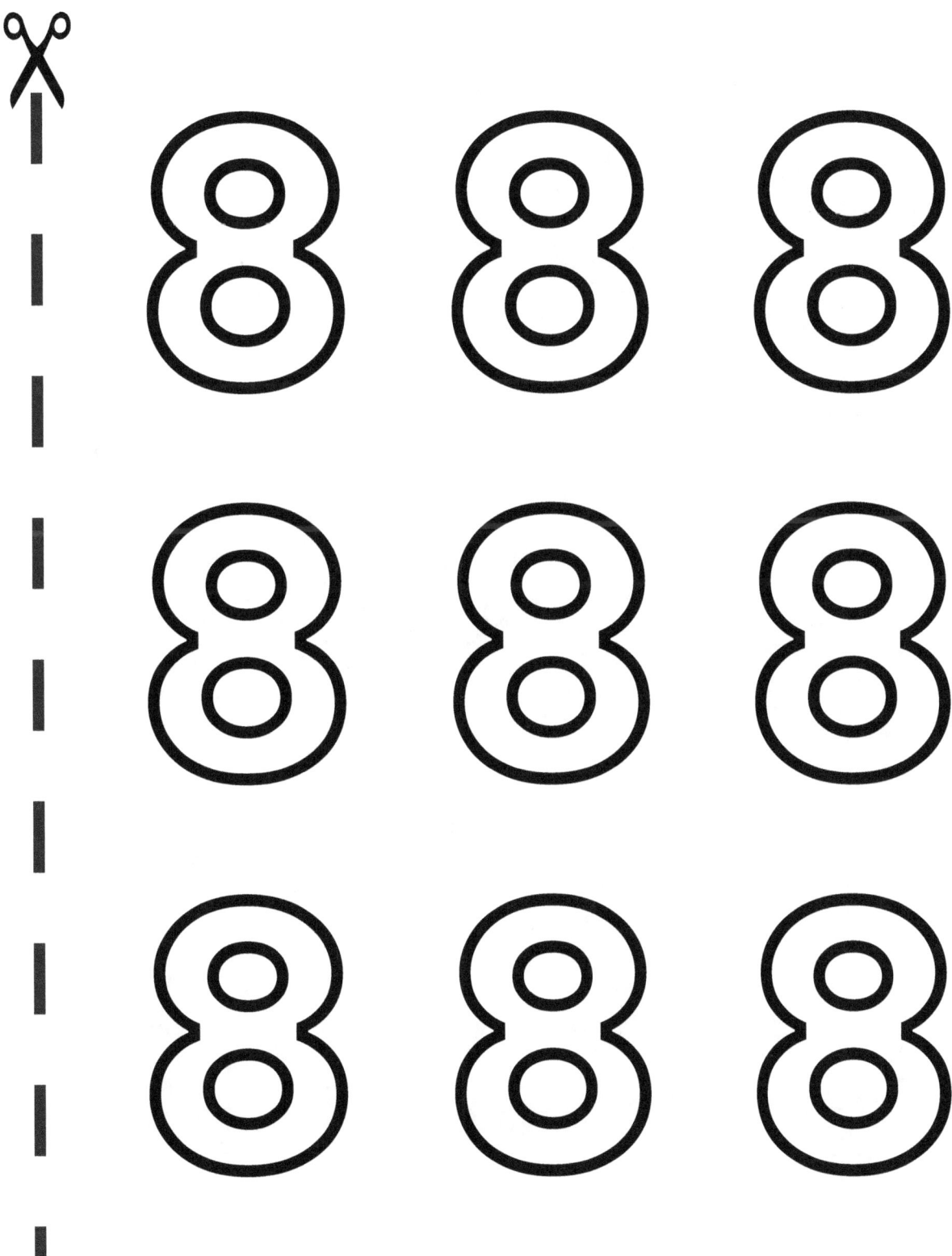

THIS PAGE INTENTIONALLY LEFT BLANK
FOR BUILD-A-JERSEY ACTIVITY

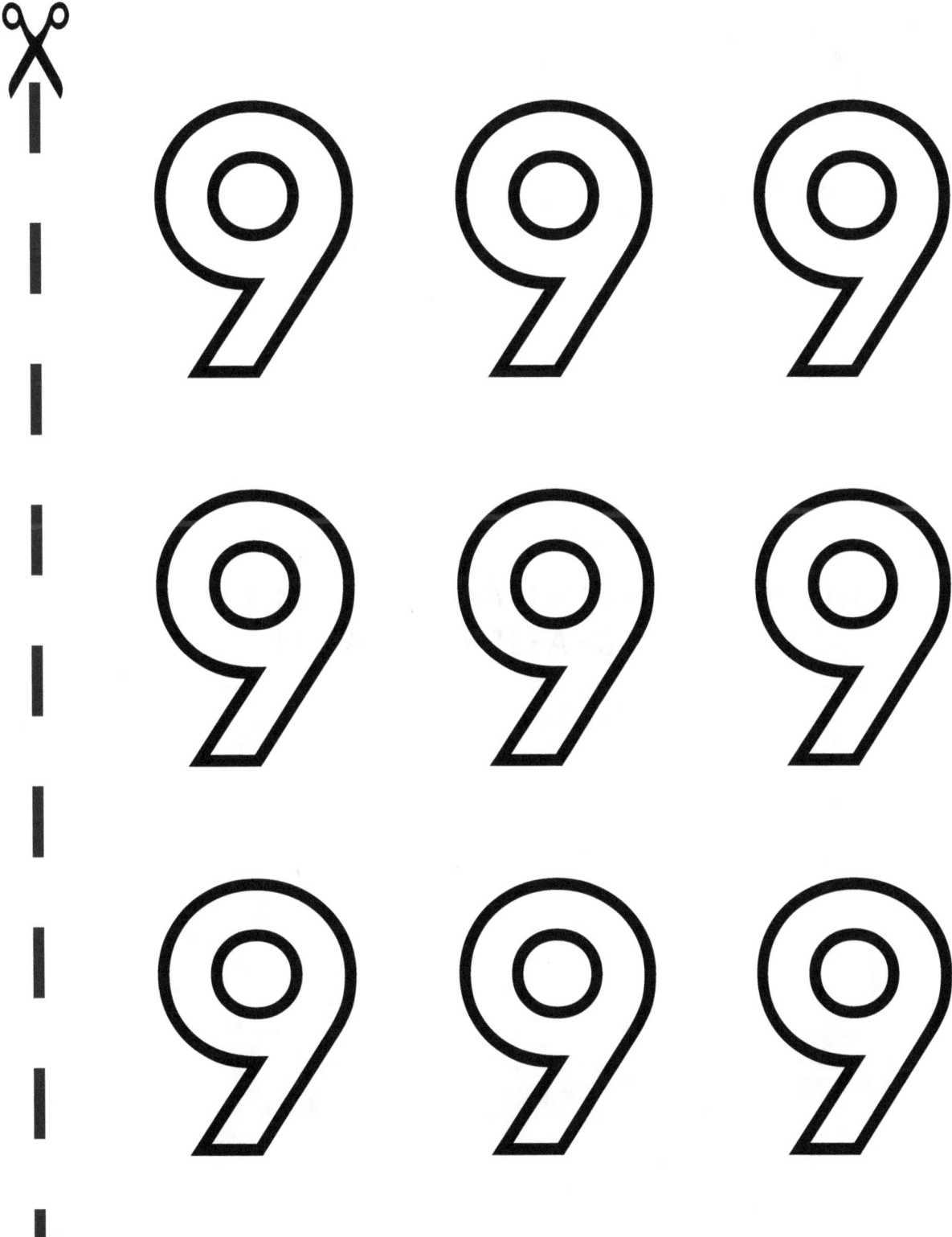

THIS PAGE INTENTIONALLY LEFT BLANK
FOR BUILD-A-JERSEY ACTIVITY

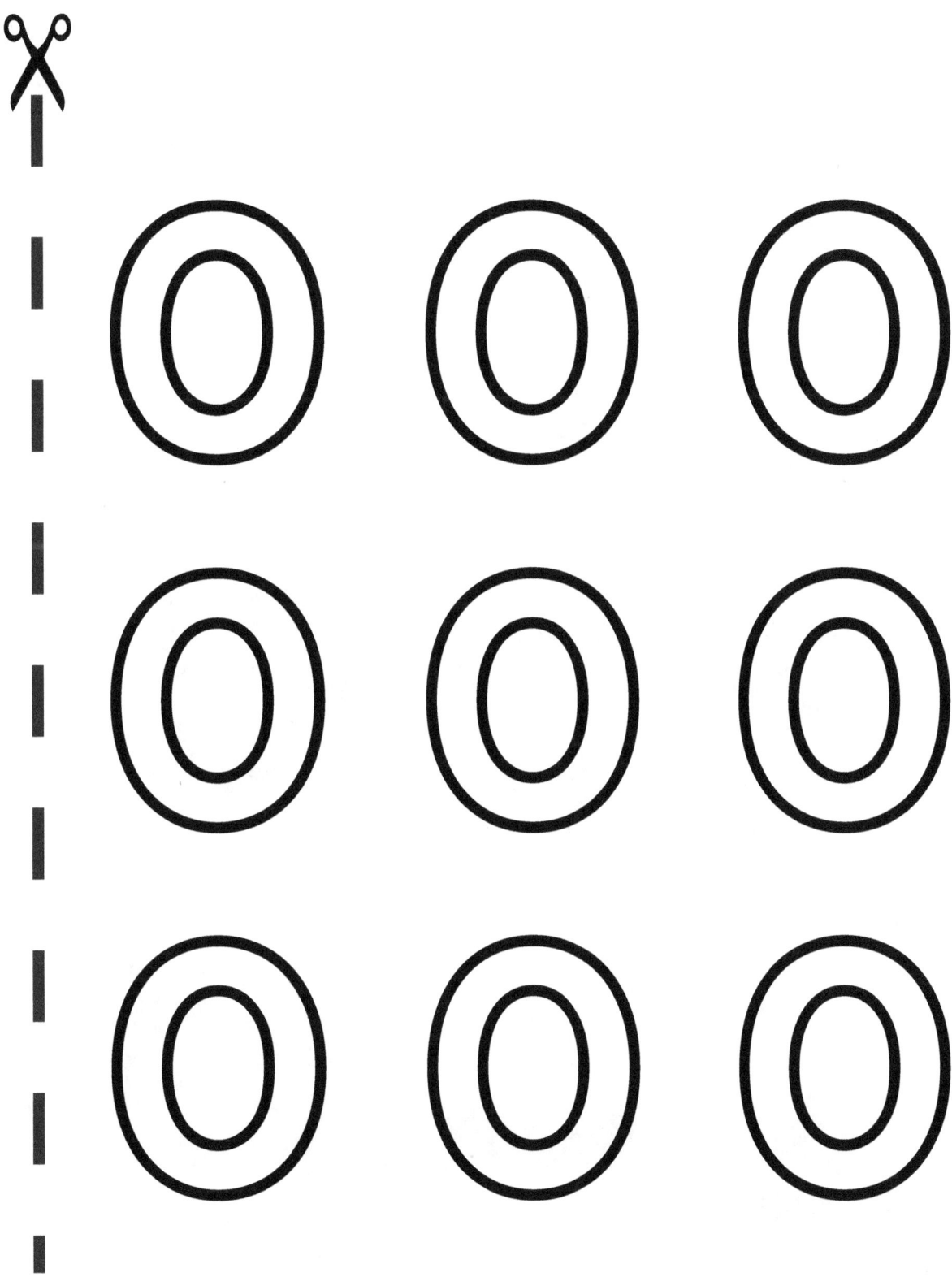

THIS PAGE INTENTIONALLY LEFT BLANK
FOR BUILD-A-JERSEY ACTIVITY

ACTIVITY ANSWERS

GIANT FIND-A-WORD

CROSSWORD

ACROSS:

1. JERSEY
5. DRAW
6. BALL
7. WIN
10. REFEREE
11. HEADER
13. CROSSBAR
15. HAT TRICK
17. TEAM
18. PITCH

DOWN:

2. SIDELINE
3. FULL TIME
4. GOAL KEEPER
8. RED CARD
9. PENALTY
12. BOOTS
14. SEMI FINAL
16. KICK OFF
19. GOAL
20. ANTHEM

SPOT THE FOOTBALL

16 BALLS

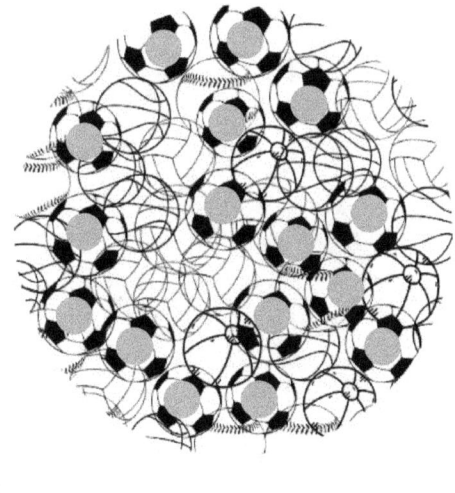

SCORE THE GOAL

SCORE THE GOAL

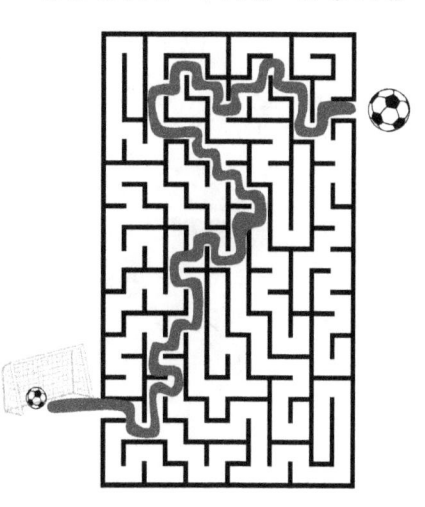

www.ingramcontent.com/pod-product-compliance
Lightning Source LLC
Chambersburg PA
CBHW081501040426
42446CB00016B/3345